SOWING SEEDS

By

C.D. Johnson
―――――――――――――――――――

C. D. Johnson Sr.

Sowing Seeds

Copyright © 2013 by C.D. Johnson Sr.

All rights reserved. No part of this book may be reproduced or transmitted in any form or by any means without written permission of the author.

ISBN 978-2-01300-010-9

Published by ASG Publishing 2013

C. D. Johnson Sr.

Sowing Seeds

Introduction

By C D Johnson Sr

For those so blessed, a heart deep cognizance secures our core beliefs. Assembling who we are, we need prompts that temper our hurtful words and actions. We pray to live daily as thoughtful people but our truth threatens to reveal us as less. Understand that the control over our child-like responses is the first test of our faith. We are still just people of the clay and our mission remains to learn and be better. But learning is sometimes slow. I have heard people call the small voice inside us as our feelings of conscious. It is more an opportunity for the lessons that we have learned to service as our option. For me I can hear the teachings from my mother, the talks with my father and a list of love ones who cared enough to help me to reach out for my blessings.

This work of writings is to fortify these options using the comforts rendered by the holy bible. Here using the word to germinate our processes in advance of our actions. To give us the power to digest the difference between the person we are in fact and the person we see in the mirror. The Holy Bible was given to us to provide sight beyond our gaze. As creatures of limited focus, reminders are most certainly a blessing, well, at least for me.

The opportunity is extended for us all. Even those who cannot yet see can be blessed to grow in the perfect light. As believers, we are simply to sow the seeds of faith and the Father allows us to grow. Sowing seeds for the world is the work of the blessed but the need for growth originates from within.

Sowing Seeds

About the author

Sowing Seeds

The author was born Clinton D Johnson of Washington, DC. He was born to loving Christian parents from the south eastern states. Clinton was educated by the Holy Bible and life in the working mans' streets. His education of this station started early and rendered hard. His lessons were heightens serving as an eighteen year old at war. The favor of our country itself would be unrecognizable now but some changes are fortuitous. This work speaks more of the growth of the man and his being blessed by the Father. He has ample room for further growth but growth is now in progress as all can be done with GOD.

This work is the second of the authors' coming to life. The distance between where he is and where he began makes clear that the Lord will come to your aid no matter

C. D. Johnson Sr.

where you've fallen. This work prays to shorten your time loss and lengthen your joy in praise.

There have been a number of health issues which provided testes but the Lord has demonstrated that sight comes in many forms and that courage has many sources.

Evangelist Mary Price

Acknowledgements

Sowing Seeds

I wish to acknowledge the love and blessings of GOD our Father. There is thanks to many but the long suffering heart of our savior is the creation of love and my reason to be better. I take this opportunity to thank the friends and family who provided their shoulders for the support of this one so in need of help. My elder child, Delan A. Johnson, declared my back covered in the way that only someone who has your back can do. Thank you to my siblings,

Debra Kelly and Angell Jacobs, with all love. To my god-child

Kadari Ali and grandson Delancy S. Johnson, you keep me strong.

Evangelist Mary Price has been instrumental in my understanding of the

C. D. Johnson Sr.

holy word and the righting of this vessel.
Along with the love of my children, who
are my resolve to smile, I've been able
to taste the blessings of my growing
faith. The driving force for this project is
my service to GOD, installing me with
my protective mission for all children. I
pray for their blessings in the light as
they grow from seeds sow.

Sowing Seeds

Sowing Seeds
Table of Contents

Page numbers

2 All in a Dream
4 Am I There Yet?
6 Angel
9 Being Brave
12 Bloodline of Relativity
15 Buried Treasure
17 Chameleon
20 Change
22 Children of Cain
24 Circle
27 Concession is not Surrender
30 Cry with me
33 Focus
36 Help!

Sowing Seeds

38	I call you Esau
42	No Greater Love
44	Sheep of Babylon
48	Sincerity
51	Spiritual Discernment
54	Subliminal Mines
56	Switches
58	The Allure of Woman
61	The Emasculated Man
63	To Know Love
65	Understanding
67	Unleavened bread
69	Wandering the Dessert
72	Wearers of the Grey
74	What would Jesus do?
76	When the fascination is enough
79	When the man loves like a Mother
82	When you call her Bitch

C. D. Johnson Sr.

Sowing Seeds

All in a Dream

All in a dream, I am altered by the total
excellence of this experience

Having fondled every moment with the
eagerness of the immature

I probe lightly in my darkness without
nostalgia of before

Dream journey made perfect, without
the dread of loss

For the source of my revival has already
come to be

There must be lessons of soul survival
that I requisite to know

Some understanding from this blessing
to paint me as bettered

I'll have love for some people of this
dream all of my life

Some of them I feel I've loved before

Even our dream promises are real and
when true to ourselves

C. D. Johnson Sr.

Each imperfect response denies our
grown and never defines a wiser course

You may feel comfort watching your life
if it were a movie

That's when the visual becomes
tangible and necessary for breath

We require all that is now and even
more for tomorrow

Abruptly, the tasty dream is melting and
the lights blink on to reality

A new census has me listed among a
grouping I don't know

My learning is now much older but so is
my form

And neither my learning nor strength of
form satisfies that I had hoped

Disbelieving that the life I pasted is the
life I have lived

Omission leads me mouth the label fool

Sowing Seeds

Am I There Yet?

I stumbled onto my understanding
Without strategy or knowing
Merely tenure with this life
This face, I've seen it before but not on
me
I understand I am no longer the sun.
My light grows fainter with each beat of
this heart
There are others in my life that I revolve
around now
And I am pleasured for the opportunity.
I want for things still but not so much for
myself
More for those I love and those I can
learn to love

We all began in need, fearful and crying
When you are in need, fearful or crying
Open your hand and your heart
A closed fist cannot provide or receive

C. D. Johnson Sr.

It can only be a tool for the ignorant, a
path for the foolish
The unfortunate response of those who
are afraid
When change is the missing piece
A single piece may be all you need
Sharing an experience is what gets us
thru the void
The greatest gift you give is you
The pain of others will always link to us
The route may not be direct but true the
same
We're only part of the greater whole
Love for self must be extended to others
to return to you
This lesson demonstrated to me early
and often
It has taken a full lifetime to digest
Am I there yet?

Sowing Seeds

Angel

We endure our trials leaning on prayers
full portion of eases

The yen and yang of this life denotes
that there are blessings still

Some learn to love with all they are but
not everyone

Growing pains make us fearful and
protective, to our fault

It is spiritually schooling to study senior
couples

You'll see the lessons of their lives,
accentuated by their weathering

When caring for your mate is the
mission that makes you clean, you still
do great work

I know this coveted godsend as having
an angel

C. D. Johnson Sr.

This gift of love is painless to crave and
so frightening to live without

Hearing a familiar voice conveying
strength to yours, nurtures valor to your
tone

The shaking hand that you hold to your
heart gives you strength

But first, you must suffer the need to be
the angel

Your spirit must be correct to both
provide and receive

Greeting this change is awkward and
reeks of the surrender of our dreams

But hope is everlasting for those who
hold fast and a dream for those who fail

Witnessed your mothers' aging, future
image of yourself

See your father struggle but you fail to
catch his fall

Sowing Seeds

Our clay pots raddle and crack, in time

With time, we'll need the aid of others,
even more so than today

If your angel blesses you, you have
more than aid, you have love

C. D. Johnson Sr.

Being Brave

Self-germinating bravado, budding
centuries before the beard

When n*aivety, formed the shield* from
where we hide and seek

The young, as the foolish are innocently
unaware

You can whistle to disbelieve your
danger

Trust ignorance to stave back the
monsters of your fear

But whistling for your spiritual life smells
overtly of a fools' bouquet

Without the knowledge of where your
strength lays

The sound from your lips is all that you
have

Ambiguity weights our loft with a
mountain

Sowing Seeds

This life is too dense to digest your learning with the days that you have seen

The strong are not made strong by their muscle or by number

The strength comes from faith in the answers they've been made to know

There is a learned focus, direction comprised of his gift for all

Commitment of spirit is in total

Total commitment replaces fear with treasured opportunity

We stride empowered though belief made self-fulfilling

The power we relish is the power GOD gives

If you believe, fear has no power on your walk in clay

We could exist in fear molding a waste of these days, never living one

C. D. Johnson Sr.

The touch of these bodies can be false
idols of their own

Sensations become addictions,
seemingly garnering the happiness we
seek

Protecting these moments will cost us
more than we know

When thought is the last thing on our
minds

These treasures age angrily before us

These vehicles are created only for our
learning

To cling to the joys of this station
exposes how little that we've learned

You were not carried this expanse just
to be set aside now

We have not yet arrived but are brave in
that we are on our way

Sowing Seeds

Bloodline of Relativity

You don't look like me but your features dictate my scene

Between us, we meticulously devise motives for misgivings

We employing skin shade as invincible evidence

And our past as our undeniable proof

We know when we are right

Trust remains rebuked as a condemnation of self

We're educated from different volumes of our own books

It's really about who's doing and who's being done

C. D. Johnson Sr.

As in the teachings about Esau and his twin
Jacob, symbiotic predicament

Life challenges begin within the womb

Labor of the indentured, fortifies the free,
bounty by position

Torture of the money changers makes
smiles within the controlled, joy from ill

Each side willing to end the world, rather
than advance to a fool

Can the purchasable rightly have value?

Can the lifeless contend with a soul?

It is unfortunately conceivable to waste this
learning

Within these national walls dwells a
paradox of our belief

One faction worships the green of the
dollar, its dominant above clay things

Sowing Seeds

Yet they fail to take notice that only in GOD
we trust and the past is not a blessing
forever

The near-compensated loss sight of
themselves

Birthing a fools insatiable pursuit for clay
things

Stuff to validate their worth and station

But things can never be your salivation

Our earthly proximity beckons beliefs
where we fear

Beloved, enrichment of the many begins
with our love of the ONE

C. D. Johnson Sr.

Buried Treasure

I was afforded a gift of affection, yet
collapsed by the spell of the package

The flawless ribbons and bows tied
knots in my focus

Perfect lines announced a vision that
made tears in my view

All proportions were formed with
flawless measure, I knew nothing to
change

Armed with the embodiment of
surrender, while leading the dance

It is understanding that must surrender;
this time must not be lost

My true gift sparkled with brilliance, all
without my notice

Its warmth, the sensitivity I needed but
the package proves distracting

Like my unspoken necessity for breath,
suffocating decisions take my strength

Sowing Seeds

The gift of affection could be only for that moment

But a moment may be precisely what I needed

The package is sure to weathering because that's the way of time

But my gift remains a gift forever, a treasure never buried

Overtly is the fashion that we respect our gifts

The cost of that which is free, weights more for some than most

We are not to past judgment for issues not our own

Just live thankfully for our treasures reveled

Chameleon

Invisibility can be a protection for the
warrior or a hiding place of those who
are not so brave

Melding into your environmental
circumstance can promote a disabling
crutch

Soon your resistance takes too much,
when we can always hide

Our lives and the gift of growth is
validated by the certainty of our death

The vulnerability of our breath self
engenders need to clutch where there
may be straws

The deep respect for that your soul
believes, never needs to be sought

There are others we label as
overzealous to compensate our lack of
zeal

Sowing Seeds

For the chameleon, to be unseen marks
his brand of flight

When standing his ground reads as
unwise, not being noticed may be his
option

This may not always by an option for
you

The person with love protects that they
love, no matter the exposure

We are the children of the Living God
but these bodies are not forever

This existence is for our service to the
Lord, fathering the growth of his children

It is natural to feel the fear of harm but
let no harm make you fear

We are reduced to chameleons when
we hide from our actions as Christians

Fearing the unknown for the sake of
security, is as a child's dread of the dark

C. D. Johnson Sr.

A child's closet monsters lose their
menace when there is light

As so for us all, where ever God dwells
there is light

Sowing Seeds

Change

The mother of apprehension abides in
how we change

Amendment to that we know, sources
stress to make us mad

Child-like illusions of continuance is
festered from our norm

We believe that if we don't
move, the world remains in
place

Our fear of unsettlement is
another test of our belief

But even during our bravest moments,
dogma drives our boat

Our aim is for the rocks, when we strike
at those who protect our backs

Abused loves ones, hold on to their love

C. D. Johnson Sr.

Even when you're the root of their abuse

Their affection will not allow connections
to be severed; they live dogma of their
own

Revolution feels like too daunting
without our direction charted

When hearts have been invested, we
can't conceive our feelings as wrong

 You simply know that repayment of
trust deserves more than the way you
feel

Let no person harm you, to your body or
your spirit

A person lashing out blindly will injure
their our life

Panic comes in many forms but all
without sanctified thought

Sometimes, all we need to do is change

Sowing Seeds

Children of Cain

Thou shall not kill

As in, you will not murder

Who requisite this commandment shred
their worth as skin

Needing an order not to murder, should
be as teaching dogs to chew

Taking dominion over the life of another,
subjects your own

But the hand strikes out quickly when
we are afraid and we are so readily
afraid

Respect is the buffer between our reality
and our license

Where we are and where we're allowed
to go

Gaining respect is more testing of some
and more than impossible for others

C. D. Johnson Sr.

We were educated to let punishment fit
the crime, an eye for an eye no more

Wisdom preserves small matters to size
but we are not always wise

When we venture to take too much from
another

Much, will be rendered from ourselves

We can be proper fools of the moment

Taking no notice beyond right now

But there is more to our absolute than
fragmented courage

With no regard for where you've come,
this can be your shining

Redemption is as near as your knees,
be welcomed to Gods' embrace

First never steal and you own no life for
taking, not even your own

- 23 -

Sowing Seeds

Circle

Surround your soul with the attributes
you admirer

Cherish emotional pillars we lean on
without regret

We are not mutually all things to one
another

But our dependent bonds are real

As in the absence you feel when your
connection is not yours

If you are a soul of stout convections, a
band of like

persons is forming to call you friend

To be thought of as friend is an
empowering place to be

There can be nothing greater without
first owning friendship

We function best, without giving
ourselves notice

C. D. Johnson Sr.

To protect us from perceived attacks in
the air

The attacks are real but our protections
are in different hands

We find strength in our circle because it
reminds us that we're not alone

But relaying on aid from the source of
your concern is much like looking for
your prison to make you free

This detour is only lasting harm when
the truth has no gleam for your eyes

We are in this time together, the threats
that make us frighten are not just in
shadow

The foundation for our circle must be
God

Without the Father no number qualifies
as enough

Sowing Seeds

There's only lasting comfort in the truth
and his truth speaks eternal

The essence of your circle only requires
the number of your salvation

C. D. Johnson Sr.

Concession is not surrender

Emotion is the fuel that drives us to where we go

We often feel strongly about the things that we should not

We contend with ourselves to steer but we need help to know just where

We requite our reward that which dangles our inclusion

Included we are, both sides are ours, in victory and defeat

Our way is made self injuring and murky

While charging error to anyone else

The factions we house are our doctrines of our exposure, the Word against the world

World methods have little to lose, its flagship fosters the moment itself

We find less for us to prize and more a trapping composed of our failings

Sowing Seeds

The unenlightened find fulfillment in the available, the selfish make no investment

Feeding upon that which we touch will find hunger before contentment

The manna foreseen in our mind lives only there

Inevitable, when the "grapes" we pursue are not within our grasp

The touch of the hand losses luster when we reach, failing to first engage our heart

Sensation alone cannot carry us to where we covet to be or make us coveted

Thankless children, we trust our blessings are a part of our legacy

We arrived with a voided core to be filled by our learning

C. D. Johnson Sr.

But no knowing is possible for one who will not be taught

Teaching never begins with its lessons

Conceding limitation makes room for our growth, limiting our growth concedes our surrender.

Sowing Seeds

Cry with me

Stumbling thru the night, the chilling rain
blows cruel discomfort on to her old
bones

An elder lady drags her ragged cart of
mismatched wheels and growing burden

She expends the little strength her aged,
enfeebled form can muster

With her ownership of the world in tow,
the nearness of her damp shelter
heartens her resolve

She gives thanks for the small pleasure
of safe arrival but being safe is not
always small or certain

The founded food will return her
strength though the wear to her essence
is exponential

You may not have this child of your
Father as your kin, yet you do

The warm, well fed nights you live never
mark you as better, only gifted

C. D. Johnson Sr.

Before your proclamation of hard work
miss-labels a person without work as
less

Understand the source of your fortune;
the reasons for your blessings are not
you

Provisions for all are retrieved thru
sharing hearts

This may not be a comfort to you,
knowing the distress of others

But if this is all new to your
consideration, your mission is
anguished

We know that not everyone feels the
links of family pain

How easily we fool ourselves as to our
work, touting the grand things we've
done

Sowing Seeds

The trials of our clay kin are not theirs
alone

If you feel their challenge, let us cry out
together

Crying defects the reality that we don't
know what else to do

But tears alone will never vanquish our
ills or respect the plight of those in
sorrow

If this notion asks of you too much, I'll
weep for you

C. D. Johnson Sr.

Focus

Focus is the disciple of the learned, the product of believing

Yet, even the fierce need certainty before leaping into the fire

Certainly is the armor you required for your life but only thru eyes made to see

Focus demands recognition to be sentient

We should know that this blessing makes us grander than we've seen

Giving all is reserved for those without hope or those without fear

Have great faith in living in the latter; fear is never your hope

The book of Job speaks of an *enduring* spirit and certainly

He lost all the rewards a clay man may treasure

Sowing Seeds

Job focused his love and service to
GOD, the benefactor of all

While the clay questioned his error, he
prayed

While friends challenged his life, he
prayed

Job knew his heart had never strayed
from GOD

Job knew GOD and that all with GOD is
good

The life of Job was again rewarded,
more over than before

But this was never a test for Job, more
over the illustration of a focused believer

Understanding Jobs' focus under
Satan's attack, sets a standard for
GODS' children

We can never access the worthiness of
GOD's plans

C. D. Johnson Sr.

Only the heartfelt, focused response
believers muster under ordeal

Sowing Seeds

Help!

When your dogma defines my future,
I'm resolved to your past

We reside within confusion justified by
convenience

It gleams expedient to keep our head
down and follow the tail in lead

Accommodating to our fear, lifting hands
are most often bitten

Learning trust at the nipple was natural,
the first gifting we receive

Is this is lack of options or is this the
time we know our place?

Remember yourself as helpless, still
truer than you know

We strain to show strength that we've
never had

We requisite to show improvement,
even when this is not true

C. D. Johnson Sr.

Dependence on true love is not to
depend at all

It's the way we learn to give

Beloved, find love in your part, be help
to all you can feel

Be a champion in your home

Moreover, be the good child to your
Father

Do not worry that you may stumble;
GOD's help is all around you

Sowing Seeds

I Call You Esau

We descend from wonderful people
forged stronger than ourselves

With time, our treasured standards are
reclaimed home

Our forbearers shouldered burdens set
aside for punished beasts

Focused by fear, they tilled forward for
to struggle is to live

Besieged every hour, heroic
accomplishments define each day

But the things they knew as vital gave
them faith

Prolonged hours further disrespected
their insufficient rewards

Less than justice for their family fair

But our portions served were hungrily
received

C. D. Johnson Sr.

Reminded daily that these insufficient
rewards, could be earned by someone
else

Existing simply for survival, with time
pennies grew to bills

Small dollars combined for down
payment on a home with your name

A place to mark your safety and be your
address to the world

Now you are the heir of the transfer of
your family growth

When are the blessings with your name
not yours?

Time for the magnanimous sharing in
you is not the time you feel

With the pressures of little funding, this
too is a color of fear

You hold up though your family loss but
is this aid you need?

Sowing Seeds

The old family house must be
exchanged for your comfort

What else should you do when your
time of need is now?

Should you bleed decades of new blood
wealth spent for these few bricks?

Is the price you are too willing to spend
meant for your children?

I call you Esau

You find life an option with your legacy
as trade

Pain extended to gain a family base
exchanged for an effortless meal

You show no perception that the edge
you weld cuts deeply in both ways

Your family hemorrhages most for the
accommodation consumed by the
greedy

Is there a sign naming your ease to be
grander than your child's

C. D. Johnson Sr.

The same restraint of those who earned
the first dollar

Remains open to those who are blessed
in turn

Sowing Seeds

No Greater Love

Remember, once your entirety was by
the grace of another
Your experiences carefully funneled and
softened, to make you feel strong
Submitting to the gift givers attention,
trust with little option

Protected and blessed for these gifts in
your life
You may not even notice that the gift
giver revolves around you

Without understanding, you feel
cherished
But in time, you grow a joining love
Now your heart beats stronger than then
And your strength presents you your
choice of direction

There is that special gift giver love
dominating from the other prospective
The sight of your child forms a smile
unfathomable inside you

C. D. Johnson Sr.

No length is too great to defend this
blessing
Allow your imagination to travel down
this horrifying road

To save the very soul of the world, your
dear child must be loss
Loss in the most loveless and brutal of
deaths
The world you've protected your child
from and provided you with discontent

Which is the greater love or loss?
GOD, in his wisdom, delivered his child
into the hands of the unjust
Affording you a chance to live forever in
his grace
There is no need in my asking your
choice
The answer changes with the parent
tasked
GOD is the greatest love
Even when we again fail to know we are
being loved

Sowing Seeds

Sheep of Babylon

You fantasize about a pathway that
occupies you with smiles

Still, to be justly lost, a traveler must first
have known their way

You faint commitment to be spiritually
seeking purpose

But seeing demands a window

And windows show much too much

So we battle to extract each moment of
our mindless bliss

Commitments are too exacting as we
are afraid

You're unsure which singing speaks
words to fit your needs

So you pound the fools' chest, record
your mock response

Give birth to fictitious valor, ignited by
your panic

C. D. Johnson Sr.

Don't exchange contentment for
fulfillment

Blessed with the vulnerability of
innocence, targets for confusion

We learn to be alarmed reading those
who share our fate

The trust of the uninitiated is as
provisional as the innocence of Eve

Delimiting our trues gives peril a familiar,
enticing favor

We wander without knowledge of our
plight or respect for our fear

We are not our salvation, that price has
already been paid

The Lamb of the world has already paid
your way

Even though the puzzlement of sheep
paints your dull expression

You march tailing the clearest voice
using words that you cannot hear

Sowing Seeds

Our truths evidenced to be far less than
we had hoped

The days of an infants' progression are
lived to make you strong

Every first step frightens and questions
our resolve

Each question and resolution grows us
closer to the true

Close your eyes to this domain where
you cannot see

Awaken to the self you were intended

No tower you build can lift you on high

The height of the tree of life overwhelms
clay fools

We were warned out of love and our
protection

No matter that we subsist in this world of
the strange

C. D. Johnson Sr.

Even sheep are strong with the lead of the good Shepard

Sowing Seeds

Sincerity

As your mournful expression proclaims
your worship of JESUS

What does your love of this world make
you feel?

Sincerity adorns those who walk as they
speak

But a productive walk requisites focus
for direction

Too often our work in error manifested
as working ill too well

Avoidance remains the recourse for
cowards

When avoidance is an avenue, it colors
true as flaw

We may fantasize that truth is mutable
by comfort

When we need we can do better being
less

C. D. Johnson Sr.

Your debt is crafted by your hand and your word

As you allow the shoddy exchange of your gift for the fools' bowl of Esau

Giving up all for that you can do without

When the treachery of another provides you with relief, you've reveal your shame

The scope of our disingenuous failings signifies more than the fact

Every falsehood a betrayal of your self-worth

And every occurrence lessens what we could be

If you learn to understand, tears should wash over each word

And if you have no tears you have little understanding, I cry in your stead

Our strength is limited by how well we keep hold of our beliefs

Sowing Seeds

Breaches lower what you expect of
yourself and thereby yourself

When you speak in word or deed, you
indenture your soul

Repentance has nothing to do with
escape

It has everything to do with an
admission of error

It covers itself with the
acknowledgement of our wrong

When an act or word injures your worth,
grief varies by what you truly feel

To mouth being sorry has no meaning
for a lie

C. D. Johnson Sr.

Spiritual Discernment

Even those who require our health are
themselves of clay

Overtly we find love in these bonds and
treasured exchanges

They give stride to mans' walk beneath
the sun

Come, let's go to a station where there
is light enough for your eyes

The most knowledgeable thought we
have is to

acknowledge that we don't know

Let's grow from the radiance that
germinates your grasp

The essence of our origination
constructs the favor of our spirit

We have impassable boundaries
dictating the sensitivity of our touch

Sowing Seeds

If the WORD forms your comfort, veiled
paths illuminate before you

Our learning begins with the wisdom of
the source

As you seek answers for your questions,
with whom do you speak?

When you except your trusted answer,
from what source is your aid?

Follow your belief, learning from what
you've been taught

It's expedient to ape the things that we
see

Easily we speak trendy words that we
hear

When unsure, we do what we perceive
and hear as we're told

We're empowered from our beginning
but we fail to discern our strength

We breed great fear of life without
guidance

C. D. Johnson Sr.

But alone has never been our ordeal

To adorn of a shelter with roman
crosses, alone

Does not make a house of GOD

Pharisees take hold as we loosen our
clench of that which we should keep

Beloved, nothing renovates the word of
GOD

But his word must dwell within you to
guide you

The Lord is our shelter, discernment of
his spirit our water

Sowing Seeds

Subliminal Mines

We are souls of the everlasting peace

Peace comes at the expense of those
who make war

The downgrade from your template
down to a mechanized child

Attests that we still don't recognize our
coveted path

The direction, to respond as stimulated
dogs, explodes with certainly

With your emphasis for instantaneous
response, you squander your time to
think

When a discourteous remark can make
you forget that which you should not

The lack of your resolve shames the
good student

Harming the sensitivities of anyone who
walks like you, is not the way of GOD

C. D. Johnson Sr.

Guiding retorts illustrate your
scholarship

While to dispense injury shows that
which we still do not know

Control of our emotional footprint is a
key to standing erect

Striking out when the subject grow too
close brings us down to all fours

Think what you will but think before you
speak

Your words may be all that's retained
about you

Subliminal switches are controlled by
the experiences of your eyes

As learned children are to be led by that
which we've come to know

Sowing Seeds

SwitcheS

We've fantasized a brand new people

Made real by our own minds

We envisioned their supple metallic skin but
could still look like you

Their forms entice with their excellence,
most exquisite to see

Made to spec from our sex dreams, the
triviality that you seek

Their excellence made tasty by their
unknowing

Their discontent is not your alarm

We would learn them to obey with switch
control precise

That failure is met with fear, much larger
than known pain

By this yoke, a dreamed elevation by fools
beneath the ground

C. D. Johnson Sr.

This again a highlight of all that we can't
know

Our limitations complicate a greedy life, a
cherub once felt like you

Where enslavement is key to your mercy or
the illusions we create

Mindless and afraid, we swallow what we
must

Fabricating, our enormity is our fantasy to
be sure

THE GOD of all requires that love be given
to truly be love

Love is the deepest exchange there is
between our souls

There is no switch for our compliance

Without GOD you've set your switch on
your own

Sowing Seeds

The Allure of Woman

The gift of a woman's nearness seeds
your surrender

Without her touch we mourn the grief of
a thousand tears

She embodies the refuge we knew, the
haven we seek

When the darkness grew our fear, her
loving hands calm the young heart

When the young world seemed to
crumble, a maternal embrace had great
power

We relate these feelings, security with
love and it make us feel safe

No other inducement has such power of
completion and of void

To even drag weaker souls, willfully
from the heavens

The essence of woman can never be
unseen

C. D. Johnson Sr.

The love of mother and that for any
other is different by objective

But a persons' dependence can evolve
in the same way

Old Testament lessons teach warnings
about strange women

But the influence of the body exchange
lives deeper the touch

We are attracted to shiny things

Things different from us

Treasuring the shiny will afford testes
that you may not pass

We are so blinded by the twinkle; we fail
to notice that it's not really a star

Let's not further spread the propaganda,
that strange means woman alone

No, making clay mistakes is likely for us
all

Sowing Seeds

Living in treasured night is not having
the spark to burn or good reason to
ignite

Strange is loving someone who has a
different heart than yours

The trails before you, you can never
travel in tandem

Messages become obstacles when they
aren't received aligned

If the partner in your life bows to other
than you do, this is more than strange

You must believe with your soul where
you need to go

The allure for strange clay, is itself
strange

C. D. Johnson Sr.

The Emasculated Man

The world ignores your utterances, the
factual source of your offence

My concern is for the speaker, speak with
me now

The Old Testament warned of our bearing
false witness

Emasculated is the man who stands on
gossip to make himself tall

Belittling bears the stench of lies, even lies
in truth

Our elevation is a reality when we travel
within to his light

But never your brothering talked down to
fall

Problems attach to all within the splatter

Retort can be your blessing or damnations
fuel

Sowing Seeds

If you don't have the love then let your
tongue be still

The flutter of your words clouds the vision
while there is one in need

If temptation circles your pleasure by
calamity to someone else

If the bloodied knee of another causes your
spirit to soar

Then your spirit drags the ground and the
carrion may be you

Scavengers partake where we're taught not
to feed

Every clay-bound moment, be blessed with
the chance to be better

Each opportunity not taken marks how long
we have failed to leave the ground

C. D. Johnson Sr.

To Know Love

We discovered loves addiction as
receiving love's first gift

When concern for another precedes
concerns for us, there's reason for alarm

In your beginning, self has been your
centered mission

Protections made vulnerable by partial
sight

The vitals of love's connection explains
little by way of reason

The sequence of importance has been
reordered by the heart

This existence that we cling to is not the
full that we will know

We know the matter of how we live
denotes the digestion of our learning

We know that there are stars to this
heaven which we may not be a part

Sowing Seeds

We know that there is always better,
that we can come to know

We must know that with love we cannot
lose, without we cannot win

With all this we learn the depth of what
love wakes true

The long suffering of GOD provides the
path for our good travel

We need come to know the Alpha of all
that's truly love

The lessons for His "clay" are as
teaching our children to stand

Every loving emotion you lived, He's
known with you

For GOD is love

If you've known love, allow love to know
you

C. D. Johnson Sr.

Understanding

Our Lord EMANUAL, often taught in parable

Exposing the extents of where we've failed to learn

His fashioning of our lessons were never intended as code

To receive from this offering is the blessing of our contentment

We must give of ourselves to receive, give of ourselves to learn

Betterment should be sole reason for our tomorrow

Each day in service to our GOD completes our life forever

Effort is the way we motivate our understanding

We build beliefs to comprehend truths we have yet seen

Sowing Seeds

Our motivation is limited by our plane of
faith

When we ignore our motivation, we
nurture our fear

Under pressure we reach out with
absolute provisional conviction

We must form as diamonds without the
pressures of the world

The wise gain value and sparkle from
His words

No other conveys the true without the
residue of self interest

Tainted messages are good messages
but they were made changed

His Holy word is the message for the
world

Our blessed understanding is the steps
from our first stand

C. D. Johnson Sr.

Unleavened bread

The foods for our lives are manifested
as varied as our needs

Fare for the flesh body fuels this form
but this gift has limits

Our service should render deliberation
but we're not that shrewd

The tenure of clay grows its importance
as an opportunity to decide

When you satisfy thru flesh
appeasement, your limits are so defined

Sensations are not your salvation;
they're the weight holding you to the
ground

If your direction is the way of GOD the
bread of life sustains forever

Sowing Seeds

Within the holy message unleavened
bread denotes long uses

This worlds' time allotment reads long
only to the young

But talk with your father, speak with your
grandmother

You may find them making ready for the
next

This incubator of souls has less to do
with now

Living for these moments dictate our
peril

Exchanging now few for forever is a
contract for the unlearned

Just as choosing to be fed by a fast
decaying loaf

C. D. Johnson Sr.

Wandering the Dessert

GOD, in his mercy, made his bonded
Israeli children free

Slavery is as a horrid, heavy coat they
wore for more than four hundred years

Warming when cold and warming more
as they blister

It was not for their comfort

Some became at ease in their pain
because real change is hard

Others had long forgotten that this was
even wrong

A believe in error can gleam true, to at
least one

It is puzzlement to some that they were
to wander for forty years

Our FATHER understands all, including
his children

Sowing Seeds

The coat of bondage can become a
function of the wearer

As with drowning, fear can force even
the brave to abandon themselves

And enslavement is a realization of fear

Those who survived, survived only in
part

They required the protection of the
armor of GOD

The Africans bonded on these shores
know well of the coat

With its wearing came the same life
letting lashings to the bodies of family

The same scars on the backs and even
deeper to their spirit

The home provided for Israel's wanders
was set apart from their capturers

They were given GODS word and the
space to heal

C. D. Johnson Sr.

There is no separate space for my
brothers and sisters

But we are well defended by the WORD
OF GOD

The same GOD of David is the one
GOD for all times

This life is not intended to be your arrival
but never your end

We are made strong in the knowledge
this is not yet home

Remove that coat, you'll find your armor
growing direction

Sowing Seeds

Wearers of the gray

Time dilutes the intensities of our lush
green days

Life's remanded to the gray weathering
of clay vessels

We frailly spend the courage saved until
we are stronger

But for those who know, you cannot be
silent

When you see a senior leaning too near
an end,   you cannot be silent

When a child cannot live as a child, you
cannot be silent

You've embraced the longevity of your
blessing, be worthy of your gift

You know how to allow direction, using
a palatable word

Your clay is no longer your strength but
lessons make you strong

C. D. Johnson Sr.

You have need to remain the quest of all
gaining privilege to your face

The mirror affords the weakness of your
plan

You are strong without your strengths
tried to the potency of your form

There are times to lead though strength
of arms

But to guide your people obliges
understandings that you should
understand

Sowing Seeds

What would Jesus do?

It flunks to make us holy, our
disapproving voice

Blistering the air, spewing venomous
lyrics able the ills of others

We mark lack of progress when we
stand aloof by our denigrating opinion

The guilty find little recourse when folly
is exposed to light

Fool like responses of elevation,
denotes a score insufficient to win

This domain garners more than a time
to frolic

A jester's devotion to his message
would mean he does not jest at all

The way for clay survival is not a
comparison of our works

C. D. Johnson Sr.

The story of a woman brought forcefully
before the Lord, with disingenuous
intent

The mob sought her stoning, to render
her passing clean

His actions were our document that all
who breathes will fail

And the response of those of God is to
demonstrate His way

Living under the sun provides
opportunity to give our family sight

Be an example in place of the judge, for
that is not your call

There are eternally eyes that watch the
way you walk, even when you fall

When there's a question as to what is
right

Simply ask your heart, what would
Jesus do?

Sowing Seeds

When the fascination is enough

The most limiting peril of our immaturity
is that we aspire to be children

We felt safe when mistakes were not
ours to oppose

Living with urgency that has no reason,
hurry that has no cause

Blessed show no knowledge purchasing
favor that does not serve

It views expedient to meld with folks we
desire to be, ape actions we cannot
know

Distinction between being justified and
being just is the evidence of our
digestion

Policing the clay sometimes makes
even mud to shine

We feel the good in life is all about
something we've done

C. D. Johnson Sr.

If you perceive that you have power,
heighten your fear

Moths to the flame as children to their
undoing

Walking the edge has a fascination
which titillates the absurd

Tempting fate denotes our willingness to
fall

There are trials which require the boy to
behave as the man

There is family who require the girl to
respond as a women

We are allotted our personalized period
of play which has an end

The fabricated satisfaction that lies to
our reality garners untruth that we trust

But this short, confused life is not our
prize

Sowing Seeds

There will be a much greater reward or failure

Only if we can perceive beyond the shiny, the fascination of all things difference

C. D. Johnson Sr.

When the man loves like a mother

The nearest we're gifted with love bleeds maternal

These angels live for these commitments, responding without fear

Endurance without regret, no requisite or pity tears

The vaginal link can manifest a perpetually open hand, but not every hand

There are those who cannot see their lives because of how they live

There are producers who solely celebrates the production over the product

They may have purpose for the moment but moments are quickly memories to come

Sowing Seeds

The dependent face of child translates
to stress from the past not joy for their
future

Blessedly, not all angels are female

There are young fathers who become
men purely by their fresh station

Within strong men there is a brutish
bridled force, their love

Feelings kept in check for fear of being
misunderstood or understood too well

But the focus of fathers should be
understood as well

When you see a good dad taking his
child to school; the hugs crush a little
tight and last a little long

Vigorously preaching, repeating
cautions for the day, but this is how they
protect

C. D. Johnson Sr.

Reacting too much to any pending ill but
this is how they love

Paternal love can be a beast unto its
self but even beasts respect devotion

The true fathers would give their lives to
protect but this often censors their smile

There are few forces as willing and none
who would give more, anything to
safeguard their line

So, how can you question the love of
our Heaven Father?

Because all about GOD is good

Sowing Seeds

When you call her bitch

If your mother embraced you as treasure,
you learn value in yourself

With the kiss from this life's first love we
learn tenderness

Securely of tenure nurtures thru the breast
of this wing-less angel

She wearing the like patience of EMANUAL

More favors from mother to child, from
heart to heart, from giver to blessed

Her womb-like shield defending your life
with hers

No matter her jeopardy, she mothers with
the conviction of breathing

This is an exchange worthy of our finest
response

Respect for the giver and those who give
should precede emotional retort

C. D. Johnson Sr.

But too often, your women's' feelings are
given little warmth

And self- control proves more than you can
manage

You strike at her heart, hurtfully, with
words of venom

Who do you see when you call her bitch?

No, she's not the same women that forged
your life

But she was your choice to bear your child

To trade mark her as your dog, barks in your
face

Is she your virginal proxy?

Has your mothers' absence left you without
manhood?

Such a wounding from her man speaks
more about you

Sowing Seeds

She will mend from your assault because
that is what she does

But, some wounds remain tender long after
the scar is gone

You show no respect for her or regret for
your limitations

 But a man has a horizon he must stay
above

Regard for your shared experience fathers
worth in you

Asking for forgiveness only has value from
one who is sorry

Only a real man can learn regret

Printed in the USA
CPSIA information can be obtained
at www.ICGtesting.com
LVHW011811241023
761969LV00002B/6